dream books

Dreamatrix Immanuel

© Copyright Sheri Hauser 2006
Published by Glory Bound Books LTD. Las Vegas, Nevada.
Glorybound Publishing
Released again 2016 in Camp Verde, AZ
SAN 256-4564
10 9 8 7 6 5 4 3 2 1
Printed in the United States of America
ISBN 0-9779654-0-6
KDP ISBN
Library of Congress Cataloging-in-Publication data is available on file.
Hauser, Sheri, 1957-
        Dreamatrix Immanuel Sheri Hauser
        Includes biographical reference.
1. Religious/Prayer.
2. Charismatic interest/Dreams.   I. Title
www.gloryboundpublishing.com

Dreamatrix

Understanding your Dreams

By
Sheri S. Hauser

Glorybound Publishing
Camp Verde, Arizona
Released 2006
Released again 2019

Letter from the Author

Dreamatrix Immanuel walks into its purpose under its own power. The word matrix means 'mold' or womb. It gives the implication of being something that provides a place enabling formation around a template. When the dream is brought into its womb, it becomes a mold leading to a birth of something new. By the light of the Holy Spirit sent from God we can experience Immanuel: which means 'God with us'. The word is found in Isaiah 8 and refers also to a child what was born as a sign that God would release the people from the oppression of their enemies.

The Holy Spirit is the night light we use to read our dreams. Welcome to the birthplace of dreams. When there is a joining of His words with our prayer, there is a birth of a vision that becomes empowered. When the dream is birthed from the marriage of ideas; the merging of our spirit with His, it grows to the point that it begins to walk on its own.

Let me show off my baby and may you give birth to your own. Hallelujah, He lives! He lives to indwell! I heard my Lord when I heard my dreams. I met my Lord when I laid them at His feet. I fulfilled them when I held out my hands to receive them back from Him anew. With joy I release to you my Dreamatrix Immanuel because God, is indeed with us. As He has given signs in the past, He continues to live showing signs today. Isaiah 7.14.

May you experience His presence a new as you learn to understand your dreams in a fresh light.

Sheri

Introduction

Everybody wants to have fun and dreams are a lot of fun. They are riddles given into our minds. Like the message written on the end of a Popsicle stick, we have to eat the ice cream to get to it. We are uncertain who is behind the messages, but nobody can deny that they play games with our minds. Is it our own subconscious mind, a reaction to our environment, or an attempt from a source outside ourselves to speak to us? Are our dreams an attempt of our mind to put together the pieces that we are unable to piece in the daytime? And, what about dreaming about those who are passed on: Does dreaming about them mean that they are attempting to deliver a message to us?

Many times, it seems like we are playing child like games in our sleep. We play 'Life' or 'Pick up Stix'. They have a cartoon quality about them that is impossible to replicate in real life. We jettison from cars to boats to outer space easily. People are called in from several years of our life and end up in the same room. Time and space is immaterial in dreams. We may all of a sudden be beautiful or fat depending on the story. And, what about nightmares: where do they fit into our lives? Sometimes the creatures in the nightmare become so real that they pull people out of bed. I have three friends who have been pulled out of bed in the midst of their dreams. Still, others have been choked, bruised and injured while they sleep. What's with that?

These dreams don't seem like games, but an attempt to scare and harm those having them. And, the individuals have no control over their sleeping visions, or certainly, they would stop them. Are they at the mercy of an outside force, or is there some deep seated evil within their personality that is coming out at night?

This book is a light hearted look at dreams. As I have studied and interpreted thousands of dreams, writing 14 books to date, all from dreams, I am about as close as it comes to being an expert on the subject.

Enjoy the book, learn to interpret your dream, see how to avoid nightmares, and gain insight into what they mean for you and others. Have fun at this adult party where kids' games are played.

I. Neon Signs

Dreams come like threads into our minds. We need to figure out how to weave them like the fabric on a lawn chair, to make a place where we can sit. They are a web, but not one meant to capture us. Remember, they are given when we rest. Only when we figure out how to not get caught up in the web, but sit on it, can we rest.

Dreams are usually pictures, but sometimes they can be only words or impressions. Generally there is a story that is told and we may be part of the story or a bystander. Sometimes we manipulate the dream while we are within it as if we are awake and able to change the outcome of events.

It is as if a screen is dropped down in front of us and we watch the pictures without being able to direct the events. We are given a movie. Sometimes, we become tired after a dream because it is as if we have lived it. Other times we dream about people we barely know and the dreams are erotic, so we wonder if it will lead to illicit affairs.

Everyone dreams, but we each have varying degrees of being able to remember them. Dreams are like impressions into our brain; like a wood burning set. They are impressed into our skull. I think of it like when we go to a concert and our hand is stamped: some stamps are clearer and leave a deeper impression than others. All of us can remember a dream we had as a small child because it has left such a deep impression on our brain.

Dreams put us in touch with an area that we can't touch when we are awake. They tell us about our sub conscious state. We have three parts to our matrix. We have a mind, a body and a soul. The mind is what we use to make decisions with.

Usually, we direct our behavior with our mind. The body is what we live within. You know, it is that part of us that each of

6

us tries to change so that it looks better. We nip and tuck it, bathe and clothe it, exercise and excuse it: our body. The soul is often ignored. I have found that the ones that are the most in touch with their souls are those that have touched death and come back. Anyone with drug experiences can tell you about his soul because he has met God.

Those who have fought the demons of depression and suicide will tell you about the spirit world because they have met it face to face.

Dreams come to us from a place we know nothing about and bring us to a place we know less about; the place of beyond our imagination; a place of the spiritual nature. I dare you to meet this place with your consciousness. For, what I encourage you to do is bring the sub consciousness of the spirit world to the conscious.

Dreams are one of our connections to God. When we learn how to convert that energy into usable forms, we can use it in our houses. There needs to be an energy conversion for us to be able to connect the messages for daily use.

If we have no control over dreams, then they don't come from us. We all have dreams that we would rather not have. Why would we put ourselves into a place we hate? We wouldn't. I maintain dreams come from the other side: the spirit side of the world we live in. God is the one who gives the dreams to us.

There are over 100 references to dreams in the Bible. The New Testament starts and ends with a dream. Mary was given dreams telling her to birth Jesus. Joseph was given dreams telling him to hide Jesus from the wicked rulers at that time. And, remember, Pilot's wife had a dream about Jesus when He was on the cross telling her that He was a godly man. Pilot responded to her dream and washed his hands of the blood of Jesus in front of the crowd.

So, I encourage you, if you are curious about your dreams, to consider this as an option. If God spoke to them, why wouldn't He continue to speak to us today?

I maintain that He is speaking, but we don't recognize the impulses because we don't know how. We know that they are coming; because like sitting on an electric fence, we all know that the dreams we are having mean something, yet we are not sure what. I do....let me roll the carpet out for you.

If God created the world, then He is everyone's Father. And, if He is everyone's Father, then He cares. Is it far fetched to think that, as a Father, He would care about what we do?

But, to think that He would care enough to give each of us impulses into our brains to tell us stuff is pushing things, a bit, you say.... Keep listening.

We all know who our mother is, but none of us can be sure who our father is. Why? We can't be sure who our father is because he provides the seed, but doesn't give birth to us. The mother has to stay with us until we are born, but the father doesn't.

How do you know that God isn't your Father in a spiritual way? If there are only two fathers; the father called the Devil and the father called God, then how do we know who is ours?

I have studied dreams extensively for the past five years and have not found one dream that I felt was from the Devil. I believe that all dreams come from God. I don't think He turned over this realm to the Devil.

So, I don't really think it matters whether or not a person is a Christian, claiming God as his Father, for God to speak into his mind with dreams. Remember, Satan did not create the world. He is not the father of it. We give him far more credit, sometimes, than he deserves.

Dreams

Dreams are given as pictures into our mind while we sleep. It is amazing that when we are asleep, it talks. Everyone dreams. Some dream more than others. I have even seen my dog lying asleep on the kitchen rug, looking like he was dreaming running after a bunny or something. His voice wines and his little legs start to move like he is running. It certainly looks like he is dreaming.

And, nearly everyone has had dreams where they nearly wet their pants. My brother got up once and went to the bathroom in the closet thinking it was the bathroom. What is that about? Certainly, he must have been dreaming.

And, there are times when we wake up in a fright or screaming having entered into a story that makes our heart pound. How we never loose who we are even though we may be at a different age while in the dream. Sometimes we float over the dream; even hovering over ourselves while the movie unfolds on the screen of our mind.

This book is not meant to be a cook book on dreams because it is impossible to cook up a recipe for your dream. What enters into your mind is as individual as you are. But, what this book attempts to convey is that there are similarities with dreams and that they can be figured out. I know. I do. From where I sit I can count 15 books I am writing; all from messages I received in dreams. You are welcome to read many of them on-line under the web site www.fordreamers.com.

It would be silly for me to defend the aspect that dreams are important. Certainly, most know of situations where dreams provided guidance to people averting them from a hazard, providing direction to a great invention, or helping to solve a problem they were facing. Most people I talk to about dreams have an experience where they followed a message in a dream with a positive outcome.

II. Now playing: Truth & Reality

A dream is a sign.

I usually have about five dreams a night. I wake up and write them down on through the night. Some dreams are more real than others, for sure. The dreams that are more real, are the ones that are meant to leave a deeper impression. They come more clearly because they are supposed to. On the freeway, they put larger signs along the road to help direct us to areas of greater importance.

The signs to cities are larger than the exit signs to gas stations. If there is an area of greater importance, then God will attempt to direct us in a big way. This will come to us in a dream with greater clarity. The problem is that we remember the dream, but we don't know how to get the message from it. Like a freeway sign in a foreign language, it doesn't mean anything to us if we don't understand its intention.

The sign isn't the destination, but that which is to be followed to reach the point of your desire. You would never think of stopping at the sign unless you need to refocus on it in order to see more clearly where it is telling you to go.

A dream provides directions to somewhere, but it isn't the final stop. The dream may say to turn right: do we stop at the sign or continue to proceed in the direction we were instructed?

We don't walk into the dream, but use the dream as a tool to help us keep on the right path. And, many times, one sign leads to another until we reach the final destination. Each time we are willing to pass beyond the dream; walk by it using it for direction, we have stepped out in faith. Because, we have no true assurance that what the sign says is true.

The assurance of truth lies within our belief of who provided the signs. Why would someone put signs along a road if not for those that will pass by to give them direction?

When a dream is a dream

At what point does a dream become a dream? Who knows? It really doesn't matter because the same principles apply when interpreting visions. A vision is a picture that comes into your mind while you are awake. Sometimes it moves, but usually it is a still life shot. I think of them like a 'watermark' on a piece of stationery: The picture is behind whatever is going on.

If you start talking to your visions, then they are becoming too real and you might need medication. Actually, in the hospital setting, most commonly we see those going through withdraws of alcohol having 'visions' that they actually attempt to walk into. They 'see' the bartender and ask him for another drink. They tear their clothes off and pea on themselves. It's not pretty. Usually it lasts about three days and the individual doesn't remember those three days. I would not call these dreams. They are psychotic episodes induced by alcohol withdrawal.

And, I guess if you sit and think long enough you can change the course of your thinking and 'make yourself' dream what ever you want. The other day someone was telling me about a class on 'directing the outcome of your dream'. That is a novel idea, but it doesn't hold much water because it isn't true. How many times have you dreamt about your old lover when you didn't want to?

Dreams and Goals

There is a correlation between daytime dreams and night time dreams and if we can figure out the connection, then we will get closer to what we desire. I think of daytime dreams as 'our heart desires'. My father wants a 45 foot yacht. It's been his dream ever since he owned one in his younger years. But, I don't think he dreams at night about it. It's a daytime dream.

I have a dream of interpreting my books into several foreign languages. This is a daytime dream. But, this dream is different from my father's dream in that it was a dream that I was given at night which I grasped and pushed into the daytime.

The question is whose dreams are whose? If God is the one who gives us dreams, then whose are they? Are they His or ours? Do we own them because they are shown onto the screen of our mind or are they His which He loaned us for a reason.

It's like taking someone on a date to a movie. Just because we go with Him to see the movie, doesn't mean that we own it. It is His movie, not ours.

One of the things He told me is, "What makes you think that I'm not interested in your dreams?"

I think when we are trying to do what God wants us to do, we feel that we must give up our dreams and pursue His. We hope that His ideas are better than ours and that they are designed to make us happy. But, somehow, it gives the idea of eating vegetables: They are good for us, but not necessarily tasty.

What I have seen as I pursue the subject of dreams is that God desires an interactive relationship which spans from daytime to night time. He cares about our dreams at night and at the daytime and just because they came from us, doesn't make Him discount them as a possibility. It's like your child wanting dessert. You don't deliberately keep it from him and make him eat only vegetables. I believe God is the same way; He doesn't mind if we have dessert as long as we eat our meal. It's like when He gives a dream in the night and we follow the message (that is our meal) and then we ask Him to help fulfill our daytime dreams (that is the dessert). I don't think of Him as a stingy Santa Clause, but someone who cares.

My husband and I work out of the same bank account. We pay the bills, then when we have money left over; either of us may use it for whatever we want.

Our relationship is interactive and we support the same things. There is a similarity between this analogy in that our relationship with God should be interactive and working out of the same account. We only have so many daytime and night time hours. He can make deposits into our account at night and we can make deposits into His account during the day. But, like the relationship with my husband, if I use all of the money all the time, then there is none for him. The correlation continues; in that if I only use God's dreams and tell Him none of mine, then the relationship is uneven. Or, if I forget to honor His dreams, yet bombard Him with mine, I use up all the funds in the dream bank.

What I have found is that when I recognize my night time dreams as being messages from God and talk with Him about them, He shows the answers. These dreams become pretty good ideas of ways to walk into the dreams that I have. He seems to have a way of directing me to make my dreams grow bigger than I projected. Dove Dreams Fly is the story of my night time dreams which I had during the time I wrote Coríanta. The dreams show a progression of leading. I give the dream and tell what I did to try to follow the message of the dream. Then I give the outcome which led me to build the business of Glory Bound Books Ltd.

Reality vs. cartoons

Dreams are interesting in that they come in all forms. I love them. We can fly and sail through the air without wings. The other day someone told me of a dream she had where she was a whale swimming the ocean all night. (I don't have any idea what that's about, so don't ask.) I have had dreams where I am 'outside' the dream looking in on myself while I do something. I had someone tell me of a dream where he was 'floating' above a surgical team performing surgery on him. Good thing it was a dream.

I think that if there is encouragement to be given, I would say, "Don't think that your dreams are any weirder than the next person."

Some really spiritual people have funky dreams. What I am attempting to do is give insight into figuring some of them out. There will be dreams which you will never figure out; I have many. But, if you try, you will find that you will be able to unravel the mystery in most. Think of them as the corny jokes in the bubble gum rappers; they are just riddles that need to be unwrapped and chewed on a while to get the flavor.

Dreams are impressions given into our mind. They are like the imprints on wood made by a wood burning set; the message is 'burned' into our mind. Some leave a deeper impression than others. It's like the stamps they give when you go to an out door concert. You know, when they stamp your hand as you wander around the concert? Some leave a clearer picture then others. And, some fade away, almost immediately after they are stamped.

Nearly everyone has a dream that they can remember from a long time ago. It left a 'deep' impression and they are able to recite it as if the dream was last night.

Still, others are like a wisp on your hand. These are like a concert stamp that was out of ink. I think of it like catching a fish. Sometimes when you hook him, he gets off the hook right when he reaches the surface of the water. Many times I have a dream and just as I am waking up, it 'swims off'. I am not able to 'hook' it well enough to remember it to copy it down. In this whole dream thing, there is a high percentage of fish that get away. Don't worry about it. Just try to 'set the hook' and reel in whatever you can.

It doesn't do any good to remember the dream, yet neglect to write it down. A dream that isn't written down looses its meaning because a lot of the message is in the words of the dream, not the pictures. If you don't write down the words, you will only have a portion of the true intent of the dream later on.

Timing of dream

One of the mistakes that I see fairly often is people mix real life with the dream. It skews the interpretation. When they ask me to help interpret their dream, I ask them to say the dream while

I write it down. Quite often, they will finish the dream then tell me of the events leading up to the dream and after. What they are doing is attempting to interpret their dream according to events. That is a backwards way to get to the meaning of the dream.

Let me show you what I mean: Suppose a woman who is pregnant has an ultrasound of her baby which shows that it is a girl, then that night dreams of a boy baby who drives a car. What she may be tempted to do is think that the dream is telling her the sex of her baby because she had an ultrasound the day before.

What she has done is allow events to skew the interpretation of the dream. A more true interpretation of the dream would be to begin with some questions related to the dream such as: What does a 'baby' represent?

You see, very rarely are dreams literal in language or character. They are analogies and 'pictures' of 'like' items. For instance, a baby is something that is 'birthed'. So a 'baby' could be a vision, a dream, a desire, or a plan that is brought through the birth canal to say, "hi'.

A more clear interpretation would go something like this: The baby boy could represent a 'small male' or 'small mail', driving a car could represent 'using the vehicle; the way. So, more accurately, the interpretation would have something to do with 'something new leading the way' like a new idea, or vision; a message that needs to be delivered. (like a baby)

Dreams with Demons

If my conjecture is true that dreams are messages from God, then what about the ones where we die, are injured, or have demons standing on our chest? I have had some pretty scary dreams waking up in a sweat hoping I wasn't in the spot where the dream took me.

What may be my nightmare, you may consider a mellow

dream. We all look at things differently. My nightmare may be your daily life. When it comes to nightmares, it's almost like our worst fears come to life and chase us around the room.

Often the fear takes on a character and rises to life, then taunts us. Death, destruction, and separation from those we love, and loss of the things we love the most and a myriad of other areas we fear stare us in the face as we sleep.

Let me examine with you a couple of options for nightmares. This is from my experience with dealing with dreams and interpretation for the past few years.

What I have noticed is three options for the answer to the question of why we have nightmares.

One reason is similar to us yelling at our child to do something after we have told him to several times. When we yell at him, we aren't trying to hurt him, but to get his attention so that he will do something that is important. Usually when we yell at our child who is running into the street it is because he is running into traffic.

In our lives we get into situations just like a child running into traffic, and God gives us nightmares to steer us clear of them. He paints the whole picture, giving it a gruesome ending.

It is along the line of the same reasoning that they show the gory flicks to the teens before they give them their driver's license. It is to steer them clear of things that would hurt themselves.

Another reason we have nightmares is that our mind is the playfield of the Devil. If we open our mind up to everything, then it will be open to everything, including demonic influences in our dreams.

Drugs open the gates wide open. Talk to anyone who has taken drugs and he will tell you about the nightmares. It doesn't matter whether they are controlled substances or uncontrolled ones, they have the same effect. I know because I am a nurse. I give drugs to people that are controlled, and often there are little old ladies who begin to scream about spiders hanging from the ceiling. I know that these little old ladies go to Mass every day of the week and say their rosaries regularly, so I would not say that their minds are the Devil's arena, but, by taking drugs, they open the gate of their mind to areas that unusually are closed.

I gave a patient some narcotics once for pain control and found her hysterical soon after because she thought her family had been in a car crash. The television was on in her room showing the news of a car crash and she incorporated it into her dream and it became real as life to her. The crash on television became her nightmare.

Watching a lot of violent movies and demonic looking video games can cause these thoughts to run through the mind at night. It opens the gate of the thought to give life to these entities. They take up personalities and over run us.

I think nightmares have more to do with the vividness of the dream than the content. A dream becomes scary if the 'flowers' in it are too large, too distorted, or come alive and start to chase us around. Many times, nightmares reveal to us our biggest fears…and that's it. Often, we don't know ourselves. These 'scary' dreams tell us who we are. It is like looking in a mirror and seeing our hair sticking up all over. We would rather see it lying where it is supposed to be, than messed up, but sometimes, the truth is that it isn't. The same is with dreams. Sometimes the messages aren't nice. They may be true, but we don't want to hear them, so we categorize them as 'pizza dreams'.

Buying Nightmares

It could be that you are doing things to prompt nightmares. It is worth investigating your lifestyle to see if you are encouraging them. If one third of the angels fell from heaven with Satan, then it is possible that they roam the earth to terrorize us. When we do certain activities, we open our lives up to the demons running through our mind when ever they want.

Many times, however, I have seen that there is nothing in the lifestyle to prompt a scary dream, but the person continues to be terrorized night after night with them. My response is to prompt you to ask God. "Why?"

Pray and ask Him to give you a dream that will tell you the answer. Certainly, if there are little demon creatures running through your dreams, then God, who created the world, and the little demon creatures, can overpower them for a night and speak to you if you ask. We don't see sin the same way as God does because He says that if we think about hating someone in our heart, it is as if we murdered him.

So, how can we know if we have opened our mind up to bad things if it is as simple as a thought in the wrong direction?

They are your dreams, not mine. If you want to keep them, go ahead. But, if you want to invite God to help, He will. I encourage you to ask for His help to get rid of them.

Stopping Nightmares

I have stopped demons from entering into my dreams while I was having the dream. Our bodies are likened to a house and to stop someone from robbing your house, you need someone bigger.

The problem with dreams is that we don't have control when we are asleep. Many are terrorized each time they shut their eyes and another seems to truck right in and take over their thoughts as soon as they go to sleep. So, they take sleeping pills and alcohol to try to drown out the subliminal messages. Try, as we might, we cannot control the flow of impulses coming in, so we attempt to hide from them. But, we can only call on one who is stronger to overpower the weaker.

If the demons are created by God, then God is bigger and can shut them down. They deliver 50 joules where He can deliver 200 joules, so He can run them out of our mind, just like He can run them out of our lives.

What I do is call on the blood of Jesus to cover the areas where the demon infestation is coming in. In the Old Testament, the Children of Israel were in Egypt and under the evil rule of Pharaoh, the King. One of the things that God told Moses to do was instruct the Children of Israel to sprinkle blood of a lamb on their doorposts to protect them from the Angel of Death as it passed over the land. What they did was kill a lamb and sprinkle some of the blood on the doorposts. Then, when the angel of death passed over, any houses where he saw the blood on the doorpost, he passed by. The rest of the houses each had the eldest die. There was a mass death in the land as the Angel of Death passed over the land. Even pharaoh lost his first born son that night. It was the final act by God that prompted pharaoh to let the Children of Israel go. He released them to go have their own country the next day. They went on to build the country of Israel.

The blood that was sprinkled on the doorpost symbolized the blood of Jesus because it was His blood that was poured out for us to put aside our death. Dreams are more than visions into the mind controlled by another. They are also our desires for our lives while we are awake. If we dream of having a baby, a house, a husband or wife, these are 'awake' dreams. Often, the Devil would like to 'kill' those dreams in our sleep by scaring us from trying to fulfill them. He wants to turn us back from those dreams. By sprinkling the blood of Jesus on the doorpost of your house, you prevent the destroyer from being able to stop in when he passes by. (Just like the Children of Israel because, they went on to the 'Promise Land'. We all have our 'Promise Land' which are things that we desire.

Sprinkle the Blood

We can ask God to protect us by sprinkling the blood of Jesus on our doorpost. To do this, all you do is ask. It is symbolic, of course, because Jesus is already dead physically, and His blood is of an eternal nature, so it lives on.

Here is a prayer to prevent nightmares:

Father who created all,
I am not sure why I am having these scary dreams.
If I have opened the door of my mind to the Devil,
please give me a dream to show me the entrance so I
can shut the door.
If, I haven't opened the door to the Devil, but he is
terrorizing me trying to take away my dreams, then I
ask you to put the blood of Jesus on the doorpost of
my mind. May that blood take away anything that is
opening the door to evil. Show me the truth.
Amen

III. Theatre of your Mind

Dreams as a Movie

The matrix of the dream is what the most important aspect of the dream is. Often the dream will come as small clips of visions. While you sleep, then don't seem to connect. It's like you walk along into a kitchen then your mother hands you a watermelon with a key in it and then, skipping off to school in the first grade. What's that about?

What the dream has done is to connect two pictures because of the words or the connotations, not the flow of the story. Let me explain. You mother could be someone who has taught you, like a teacher or the Wisdom of God (mother wisdom). When you enter into the place where her ideas are cooked up (kitchen) you will be given a key to learning: and we all know that we start by going to school at the primary level. And, the watermelon could have the connotation of something large and juicy; sweet, but home grown.

So, you say, "I like where you went, but I don't know how

you got there."

OK, I will take you down the road holding your hand for educational purposes:

What I do is write down the words, then attempt to define them. When I was first learning dreams, I used a dictionary to help expand my understanding of certain words.

For example, I had a dream where a coat of armor was formed on my body by the hand of God. Each stitch came as a dream, a prayer or a song I had prayed, or He had given. It was the mail between us. In the dream I ran out into the daytime. Well, I didn't realize that this knitted armor was called 'mail'.

The dream took on additional meaning when I realized that it was the 'mail' that passed on between us (interactive relationship) which formed the basis for my protection and this enabled me, dressed as a knight to walk into the daytime. (The night ran into the day when I put on the mail.)

So, you see the words mail and knight had duo meaning within the dream. But, I didn't realize it until it used a dictionary to look them up.

The other day someone told me a fun dream: A porpoise came to her as she walked into the water at night. At first she thought it was a shark and she was scared, but then, when she realized it was a porpoise, she fed it.

Now, look at the words of this dream. Porpoise sounds just like purpose. She is walking near the beach; the sea. She is in the place where she sees; her eyes are open. And, she sees this thing coming which she thinks might be bad (a shark), but it turns out to be fun (a porpoise). But, I think that the dream has a bigger meaning when you see the word as purpose. Because, for her, what she had seen as scary, became fun with purpose when she extended her hand to feed it. (It's learning about the purpose of dreams and feeding her understanding.)

Movies vs. Flicks

Don't think of dreams as fish: just because they are bigger, there is more meat on the bones. A longer, more detailed dream doesn't necessarily pack a more powerful message. Often the shorter ones pack a greater punch. They may be just the words that you are looking for to answer a crucial question. So many times I have woken up with only a few words kicking around in my head and thought, "Oh this is so simple, certainly I will remember it in the morning." Then, sure enough, I can't.

Most of the writings in Love Notes are from short dreams I received. Remember, some valuable things come in little boxes. One of the short dreams He gave me was a statement, "We're writing a book." It became the first book I wrote which turned into a library.

Imagine my surprise the next morning when I read this statement on the dream book that was on my night stand. This is an example of a little message in a big box.

Dreams come like threads dropping from heaven. Pretend that you are making a quilt and need a lot of colors; it will take many threads to weave this quilt. If God has a long message given in dreams, it might be continued for a couple of nights in another dream.

If you can put yourself in a position where you are attentive night after night, He will trust you with longer messages. Think of Him like a King with mail that needs to be delivered. If He has a message that is lengthy it needs to be delivered with the same amount of accuracy as the shorter ones.

Suppose you write down a dream one night, and then don't write down a dream the next night because you are too tired to wake up and write it down. Then, the next night you have another dream. Have you missed piece number 2 of the puzzle? Will you end up making a quilt missing a few colors? I believe you will. If you want a colorful quilt, then you need to be consistent in paying attention to all of the messages, both long and short.

Sometimes the short dreams don't make sense. Just write them down. Last night I had a dream I was wearing a red dress. The dream was about spilling egg all over me, and then going into the office. Then, in the end I clean up the dress and catch a bus.

At first the dream didn't make sense. Why was the dress red? Well, what I have done is re-address my web site. And, when I re-address the office issues, then I will be read (red) by many. Copying the detail of the color of the dress was important to the message of the dream.

The information for the books was given to me in dreams over a period of about 3-4 months at a time. I had dreams on a specific subject for a while. I copied them down, interpreted and correlated them with the Bible. Then, I would be given an 'outline' dream. It was simple. All of the books have only a few chapters, so the outline dreams have main elements which all of the other dreams can fit under.

The outline dream for Tomaseña was simple. I can remember it: All of the houses in the neighborhood receive boxes. My husband brings ours in and sets it on the table. I come in and open it. I used that dream as an outline because it has steps of action.

The first chapter is entitled 'Door'. You must bring the gift through the door.

The second chapter is entitled 'God's heart desire'. Guess who sent the gift?

The third chapter is entitled 'Filling the need'. Just like a parent, He sends something we need. A parent would sent a vacuum cleaner, not a rock CD.

The forth chapter is entitled 'The Holy Spirit'. We open the gift God has given to us. It is a gift of His presence (presents). Get it?

The fifth chapter is entitled 'Prophecy shared'. When we receive a box of chocolates, do we share? These gifts of the presence of God are meant to be shared.

And the sixth chapter is 'Prophetic prayer'. It's the 'how to' share rules.

Prolific Dreaming

When people tell me that they don't dream, I ask, "What did you do with the last dreams God gave you?"

And, when they tell me that they 'didn't do anything with them', I say to them, "If you did nothing with what God gave you before, why would He give you any more?"

So, if you find yourself in that place, I suggest that you have a chat with Him and say you're sorry for throwing that last 'gift' He sent you into the trash can. Think of Him like a real father. If your father sent you a present in the mail and you refused to open it, throwing it in the trash, then why would you question him not wanting to send another to you?

The one thing about God is that His mercies never end and His steadfast love endures forever, so you can ask forgiveness and change your ways, requesting Him to send you more presents, and He will. But, don't expect Him to send you messages from heaven if you threw the last ones away. Deal with Him in prayer, first, then put a pad by your bed and make it a place where He can drop by with a message if He desires.

Also, there is no correlation between who gets what. We honor men, but God doesn't. He gives gifts to who ever He wants. Remember, He is God.

Visions

Sometimes we use the terms interchangeably, but they are different. In a true sense, a dream is given at night and a vision is given during the daytime. To be called a dream, we need to be sleeping; whereas with a vision we can be in a 'trance like' state. Both are pictures shown on the screen of the mind

A vision comes with all of the same elements as a dream, but the person is awake when he has it. Sometimes, visions can be moving, like a dream, but usually they are snap shots. A dream is more like a movie, whereas a vision is a still life shot.

I have had moving visions. Several of the long writings that I have done are from moving visions. With concentration I have been able to focus on the vision and write at the same time. The Vacuum Cleaner Salesman from Abreas Ansus was written from a moving vision. (Look on the www for it. GBB)

Some have more visions, just like some have more dreams. Certain individuals are more visual than others. There are 'hearers' and there are 'seers'. Some are more in tune to 'hearing' things in the spiritual realm, and others have a tendency to 'see' everything.

I see everything that I write. For me to understand it, I need to visualize it, then, I can write it down. Some of the first word dreams that I wrote down were given to me as pictures of words etched in the side of a building. I saw the words, read them, and copied them down as I saw them. They were not whispered to me.

Visions can be interpreted just like a dream. They are metaphors that depict true meanings of same types of elements that a dream contains. If you are having a lot of visions, then you are probably having a lot of dreams. It merely means that the dreams are spilling over into the daylight.

If you work on learning how to interpret the dreams that you are having at night, then you will be able to make use of the visions as they come to you during the day.

The more dreams that you interpret for yourself, the better you will get at understanding the messages quickly from them. Then, when you have a vision, you can interpret it quickly. It opens a whole new door for God to speak to you in the daytime, as well as at night.

Visions are just like dreams, in that they are stimulus coming into your brain giving pictures of things that you don't have any control over. A vision that you control is not a vision, but a day dream. There is a difference. With a day dream, you desire something, or someone, and allowing your desires to direct your thoughts If you desire a certain person to have a romantic relationship with, perhaps you may dream about you and her on a desert island. This is a day dream because it is a vision that is directed by you based on what you want for yourself. The visions that I am talking about are pictures than 'snap' into the brain over what ever is in the room.

Visions are seen with the soul. That is why we are able to cook up our own visions. When we have desires our soul years for things. It becomes a question of: Who owns our soul?

If we claim ownership of our soul, then it is difficult for us to have visions from God. But, if we allow Him, He will give us visions. The issue is that, when He gives the visions, they come from Him. Of course. It's like saying I want to have a conversation with a world outside of myself, but I want to direct it. It is impossible to direct visions, yet have them be from God. He is not interested in trying to compete for the playing field of my mind. So, the real answer to the question is contingent on whether or not you want visions from God or from yourself.

Dreams and visions are the same. One is while we are asleep and the other is while we are awake. Both are pictures into the mind. The benefit of having visions over dreams is that it is easier to write when we are awake.

Just a Banana

A banana is just a banana
until you see it as something more.
A dream is just an idea, like a vision,
you have seen in your head before.
A woman is just another girl
until you make her your wife.
She's just like any other relationship you've
had in your life.

And, a banana is just a banana
until you see it as something more.
And, a dream is not a boat
until you see it come ashore.
Cuse, there's banana cream with coconut pie
And, there's grand ala mode.
There's banana boats, fantastic floats,
never tasted until tried.

And, a dream is just a dream
a picture in your mind.
A vision yet unopened, until you seek to find.
Take note of the boat that, to the island goes.
Sneak a peak and sniff with your nose.
Curiosity is on your side as you unravel
the mystery at hand.
And look for the message that has been
there just as planned.

And, a banana is just a banana
until you see it as more.
For, a banana left unopened
will never come ashore.

IV. Screen Play

Night class: questions, answers and examinations.

There are different matrixes of dreams. Just like using the same ingredients to make a cake or cookies; God can mix up what ever He wants using the same pictures but putting them in a different setting.

It will help you to understand the matrix of dreams if you think of them as 'messages'. You know; the type that we leave for our loved ones when we go to the store or the movies and want to tell them something? Some messages are short and some are long. They are personal depending on the situation. Some are intimate and some aren't.

What you need to do is write the dream down. Sometimes the dream may be a question asked in a rhetorical way. Let me explain: when you want your son to take out the trash and both; you and he know that he was supposed to do it, you ask him this way, "Did you take out the trash?"

You both know the answer to the question because you are standing over the trash as it heaps into the kitchen. It's not that you both can't see the answer, but you are attempting to point out that he isn't doing his part. God is the same way with us. Sometimes, He may give us a rhetorical question. It's not that He doesn't know the answer (Give me a break, He's God.) but it's that He is trying to point out that you are not doing what you promised you would do. So, let's say He gives you a dream about someone in Church. In the morning you say to yourself, "Why would He give me a dream about Church when I haven't gone to Church in a long time."

Do you think He knows that? Of course. But He is trying to

28

point out to you that there are things going on in Church and you are not where you promised you would be.

Talking Dreams

Then there are dreams that give the answer in 'God language' as if He spoke it. Let me show you: If He gives you a scenario and puts you in a position of responding to individuals, and then you say and think certain ways. If you write down your response, it becomes as His words to you.

Here is an example: He gave me a dream last night where there are thousands of people waiting for a Savior. I am an observer and what I see is, "There are thousands of people waiting for a Savior." If I back up from this message, then it becomes God's words saying that there are a lot of people waiting for Him. There are many who want to hear from Him; not only a few, but thousands.

This message is like one that you would tack up in the lounge at work. It is information that all need to know and He has given it to me because I care. It doesn't direct me a specific way, but provides insight into what is important to Him.

I would become suspicious of any dream where you talk to others. Just write down the words and read them back to yourself. Quite possibly they are a message to you. Remember that God is Spirit and He needs your lips to make noise. So, in a dream it wouldn't be strange that your lips would make the message that you need to hear.

This principle is kind of hard, so I will give you another one. Suppose you get a dream where you need to get out of a boat to get into another one. And, in the dream you are frightened, but the boat that you are in is sinking, so you make a jump for it.

This dream has feelings that you can write down as well as the scenario. Let me unravel it for you: the boat is your situation. You need to go from one to the next, but are unsure. The message says, "Go ahead; your boat is sinking anyway. What you are clinging to is going down fast."

It may as well be words from God saying, "Take a leap of faith and get out of your safe zone because what you see as your safe zone isn't so safe."

In the dream, you didn't say it, but you were put in a predicament where you thought the right answer. I would dare say that you have asked God for direction in a situation and this is your answer.

Sometimes, the dream gives an option we never thought of before. This is just a new direction. I have had many of these. One I can remember was given to me as a statement. 'Sheri, there is no reason to go on Television until you have something to say and something to sell.'

This was a shock to me because it was given before I wrote my first book. But what the dream was saying was that God was thinking about publicity for His project and I should be, as well, but don't seek the spot light until it is time.

Plans and warnings

If you become a friend of someone, then you share. There are 'sharing' dreams. Sometimes when my husband and I are sitting around, he tells me his plans. If dreams are from God, why would He tell you His? It doesn't call for you to do anything any more than my husband telling me about his plans in his job invites me to join his occupation.. I like these because within this category God tells how He feels. Many times, with these dreams we become children and there is a father figure who responds to us in a certain way. We just copy the words and read them back to ourselves in the morning. They are friendly messages from a friendly God.

Here are some dream hints:

Ø   If you have a father in your dream, the chances are pretty strong that it represents your Father in heaven.

It can also represent your earthly father because God can multi-channel this way. But if I have a choice which road to take, I always take the Holy Father route over the temporal father route. Usually, I can't figure out what I am supposed to do with my earthly father, so I choose the Heavenly Father because at least I can pick up my assignment and do it.

Ø   If you dream about a mother, it could represent God's wisdom because in the book of Proverbs wisdom builds her house: she is personified as a mother. This is not to say God is a girl. Last time I checked, only guys were fathers. But, there is an aspect of God's character that trains us, like a mother: He mother's us. It is our Father that gives us spiritual milk from heaven just like an infant; we suckle from His breast and feed off of what He offers. He also shows us how to 'cook' up things in the kitchen of His wisdom. He shows us how to build our houses, our lives and our families. His training puts us on track (like a choo choo train) and provides the rails that we need to get from one place to the next.

Ø   Note: if you dream about your brothers or sisters, then it could be those that are related to you in a spiritual sense. It could be those who attend your fellowship.

Prophecy

The message of the dream should move us closer to God because that is the goal of God in all of His interactions with us. The dream might reveal areas of sin. If we have been praying for God to reveal some hidden sin in our life, perhaps He will give us a dream (Psalms 51). Maybe there needs to be a change in our life. Perhaps we are off the track that God wants us to be on. He will, often, reveal this to people in dreams. If we are in a position of authority, God, often will speak to us about individuals whom are under our authority. This will provide direction what to do with them to help them to move closer to Him.

Another area where God talks to individuals through dreams is with "Strongholds". Strongholds are areas in our lives of bad teaching where have learned something wrongly, and God is trying to tell us to relearn it His way.

Dreams may be prophetic; insight to provide direction to decisions for the future. They also provide heart direction, if your heart needs to be realigned to God. The direction may be immediate, or lifelong. Remember that dreams are like boxes to be delivered to our doorstep. They have stickers on the other side of the box. This means that if we have had a dream several years ago, there is another message, if we ask God to turn it over again. We can revisit each dream time and time again. A dream may be timely with a message, but it also has a bigger message for another time. Only a message from God could do that!

Remember to come up with the message that God intends, we need to use His parameters for interpretation. There are many programs with tools to help interpret dreams, but be careful not to trip over someone else's' toolbox as we travel through the matrix of dream interpretation. God will give you your own tools for understanding your dreams because He is on your side: He cares.

It is impossible for me to interpret your dream because I don't have your tools. The only way I can help is to show you where to go to get some of your own. I have a web site with a chat room where I invite people to share their dreams and I select a few and try to help then unlock the meaning, but I don't know the answers. I only know the questions to ask. Suppose the dream has a situation where a snake enters their house and sits on the couch. I can hypothesize that the snake might be a representation of the Enemy and he has found his way to their couch. So, I would ask questions like:

Has something new come into your life?
What is in your living room that shouldn't be?

And, I might assume to presume that the enemy might have snuck in by way of the television as they sat on their couch, but I don't know if that is true. When I rush to interpret the dream for them, I mislead them taking them down my trail instead of their own. When I ask the question, I might learn that they have a new visitor who has been sleeping on their couch who they suspect might be stealing from them. You see how different the message is? If I would have told them mine, then they would have missed the intended one and continued to be subjected to a thief within their house without knowing it. But, now that they know the true message, they can make provision to get rid of the nuisance on the couch.

Be careful not to get too spiritual with dream interpretation. There are levels of dream interpretation and I am not sure that all levels are for everyone. It's like when we go to the swim pool on a hot afternoon. We are all at different levels of swim expertise, yet we can all enjoy the cool water. We are not all destined to be Olympic swimmers and it is important not to demean someone who isn't. They can enjoy the water on the shallow end with the kids. Many of the most crucial messages in dreams are simplistic and we miss the main one when we attempt to take on the high dive without learning to swim. If you are interested in the levels, you can read Tomaseña.

Helping with dreams.

Another point is that if we attempt to push out into the deep aspects of dream interpretation without clarifying the basics, then we will end up at a different place than where we were supposed to go with a bigger problem in the end. Let me clarify: put your finger on an X and Y point and move it out toward another point. This defines a vector. Now, put your finger on a point nearby the other one and go in the same degree outward. See?

You end up in a different spot proportional to the degree that you were off in the beginning.

To help you understand, let's correlate with swimming again. If you don't learn how to hold your breath with the simple strokes, what will you do when you go off the high dive and are under water for a long period of time?

There is a special problem attached to dream interpretation in that all dream and often, we can see 'evangelistic' messages embedded in the dreams of those who we work with. It is a great opportunity to share the gospel with them. What better way to share the answer to their need than by turning on the light within their understanding to reveal that God is personally interested in them by giving them a special dream. And, when your friend learns that you are interested in dreams and getting direction from God within your dreams, he will come to you to interpret his dream.

What I recommend is that you pray and ask God for direction and stall. Because, the dream isn't going anywhere and if the person is more curious, he will listen better. So, I don't help anyone interpret their dream unless they ask twice. This is just a personal rule. I figure that if they ask once, then perhaps they are being nice to me thinking I am the 'dream expert', but, if they ask twice, then they may really want to know the answer.

Then, I unravel the dream by pointing out 'possible' questions. I 'back' into the room. Even though the answer is obvious to me, it is important that the person see it first. It's like an Easter Egg Hunt; it's his dream, not yours. And just because you found the answer first, doesn't make it yours. What I do is keep asking questions which give hints toward the answer. If the person changes the direction of the answers, then I know that I am going down the wrong road and I ask questions of a different type. Let me give an example: Suppose someone has a dream he is in a Catholic Church and the Tithe basket is empty.

I begin by praying and asking God for direction, and pause waiting to see if he is still interested in the answer. If he isn't I don't proceed; I wait until he is. But, if he is attentive, then I ask him the dream, carefully writing down the words. I separate the words from current events and ask for any clarification to understand the dream.

Then, I ask questions: What does the Catholic Church represent to you?

What does the tithe basket represent to you?

Why would this basket be empty?

You see, the questions are all geared to the individual's understanding of what the elements mean to him personally. That is why I did a 'chat room' on the www; there needs to be interaction to get to the final answer.

Now, I could skip with the dream and move straight to the 'prophetic' interpretation and give it to the individual. A spiritual interpretation does not move; it drives the dream right up to Scripture and parks it where it fits. If I were to take the dream above and 'park' in next to Scripture, I would probably go to the section on tithing and where it is our responsibility to give to those who minister to us spiritually.

That is the 'bigger' message of the dream. It would read something like this: "There is an area of emptiness within the Catholic Church when it comes to giving."

You see, when I grabbed the dream and correlated it with Scripture, it became 'prophecy'. The problem with this interpretation is that it did not follow the steps in the pool to lead toward the deep end. It is quite possible that this interpretation is not for the individual that had the dream. Although it is a problem in the Catholic Church, the message should go out like a 'bulletin' instead of a 'personal note'.

The safest thing to do in order to avoid ending up at the wrong vectors when we help others understand their dreams is to leave the questions for them to answer.

It is very tempting to want to fill in the blanks when we see the assignment and think we know the answers, but it is not the best thing to do. When we rush for the answer, we only promote ourselves in the eyes of the one who came to us and do not teach him where to find his own tool box. Remember, he has a tool box, too.

Who is who in the dream?

I have seen, many times where someone encounters a child who has eyes very much like they do. With these kinds of dreams, I think we come face to face with the child in us. Perhaps we are facing unresolved issues from childhood.

If you dream about your loved ones who have died, then God is using the place to set the stage for the dream. Think of it like a stage that needs a backdrop. Dreams are moving pictures that need backdrops. If the dream includes someone who is 'in heaven' then it is like: This is the way it is when viewed from the way heaven sees it.

Another way to put it is: This is how it is in the Kingdom of Heaven. The dream is setting up an ideal situation; presenting things that way God would like them to be if He ran the show. He puts the setting of the dream at 'His house'. Certainly, they would do things His way at His house.

Another reason you may dream about someone who has passed on it because it answers a question you have regarding that individual. Suppose you were wondering if you brother resolved certain conflicts he died. This dream may be a message telling you the answer to your question.

I do not think that when we dream about people who have passed on that they are sending us messages because there is no indication in Scripture to validate that someone who is dead can come back from the dead to communicate. In fact what the Bible says is that the only one who came back from the dead is Jesus. He has left us the Holy Spirit who lives to make intercession for us. He is the one who gives messages to us from God. I think it is a stumbling block to follow directions given in a dream from someone who is dead assuming that person will lead you. Personally, I think that this idea is one of those tool boxes provided by others which we don't need and will certainly trip over if we leave it in the living room of our house. Get rid of it.

Tomato Dreams

We need to seek to follow God apart from our dreams and use dreams as a part of hearing His voice providing direction. Dreams are like tomato plants. If I am going to plant a garden, I go to the store and buy some tomato plants. Because I am not very patient, I get bushes with tomatoes already on them. Then, when I bring them home and plant them, there is a pretty good chance that they will grow some fine tomatoes.

But, suppose that I go to the store, buy seeds and grow my own tomato plants setting them in the windows until they sprout in their little boxes. As I watch them grow, some of them don't do so well and die. But, by the time it is time to move into the garden, I will have an abundance of tomato plants. And, will all of the seeds bear tomatoes? Probably not. But, let me tell you, I will have a big crop because I was willing to begin with the seeds instead of buying the plants. A dream is like a tomato pant. When we follow it, there isn't much risk that it will bear fruit. But, if we can learn to plant seeds, then we will have even more than we ever dreamed of.

And, what are the seeds? Prayer is the seeds of God's wisdom. When we pray and learn to listen to His voice in the daytime, we will have so many seeds, that we will not be able to find soil for them all. And, if we are willing to try to plant them in the windows of our mind allowing the sunshine of His presence to flow onto the words, then they will grow into our dreams. That is how I got 7 books in 3 years. They are not simply made from dreams, but hearing His words in the daytime, as well. And, is it risky?

You bet. But, does it pay off? Look at my crop and you answer the question.

Bowling Straight

I think of it like a bowling alley: we need to keep our ball rolling down the center in order to win the game. He has provided some things that will help keep us out of the gutter. It is like balloons that for little kids that prevent the ball from being able to go into the gutter. The balloons correlate with God's words coming to us. In one gutter is His word for yesterday (Scriptures) and in the other gutter are His words for today (dreams, visions and meditations). When we have both balloons then we are less likely to go into the gutter.

If we only follow the words for yesterday, then we will be stiff and stagnant, like a lake. We will not have 'flow' ability. I know people who, when they are seeking leading from God, let their Bible open up in any spot and read the words. Then, they follow the advice of these words for direction. But, I say, that we limit the responses of God when we limit His words to one book. He is much bigger than that. He speaks through creation, for instance. That isn't a book, yet we can learn things about God when we study what He has made. We study the work of the author and learn about Him. The rocks and the streams tell of His greatness and majesty.

And, I know those who do not read Scriptures and when they want direction, they ask God, and then wait for an answer. They listen to every dream and desire to follow it. But, without a standard, how will they measure the words?

The Bible was given to us as a standard; like a ruler, and we can set whatever we have up against it to see how it measures up to other words that have been spoken by God. Suppose we have been given a vision of a lion walking toward us. If we do not know the Scriptures, we may become frightened with this vision and worry. But, if we know the Scriptures, then we know that a lion is one of the symbols for God's presence. So, by knowing the Scriptures, we become assured that God is bringing His presence to help us within a situation.

Mailmen and Women

Sometimes we are given dreams and it is obvious that someone is doing something wrong. Let me give you a couple of examples:

One time I dreamt that I was with Rita and I cut her hair. She didn't ask me to, but I did it anyway. Well, it didn't look very good and I didn't apologize for it. I made excuses and walked away.

It's obvious from the dream that I was wrong. Apparently, I did something, or said something going where I wasn't adequately trained (I am not a hair dresser) or invited and 'clipped' her. Well, I looked at the dream, interpreted it, then closed it up in a file and put it on the shelf with my other papers.

A couple of months later, God gave me a dream telling me that I was bad because I wasn't delivering the messages that He was giving to me: In essence He said I was clogging up the road and standing in the way of what He wanted to do in others lives.

So, I repented, and the next day I went to Rita and asked her if I had wounded her in some way. The inference that I had received from the dream was that somehow I had 'clipped' her like a football player 'clips' someone else on the playing field. In football, it's a foul and the team gets a penalty.

I anticipated that she would tell me of some way I had hurt her, but she didn't. I continued to ask her if someone else had hurt her. To my surprise, she opened up to me, telling me about recent hurts. Then, she asked me to help interpret a dream she had. When I helped her with her dream, she received wonderful peace from the message. Because I was willing to go to her with a spirit of humility, God used me in her life to help her with some tough issues she was confronted with. She confessed that she had been clipped, but not by me and began to understand the importance of dreams in her life.

Hearing Good, Better and Best

Let me tell you another story: I had a dream that a person was lazy. What God said was that he had caused many to sin because of his laziness because they became angry waiting for him to be true to his words. Well, I didn't want to get in trouble with God again for not delivering the message, but this message was more difficult than the last one, so I made a deal with God.

I really didn't know the person very well, and I felt really uncomfortable telling him that he was lazy, so I told God that I wouldn't go to the guy and deliver the message, but if, he came to me and asked me, "Do you have a message for me?" then I would tell him the message.

Of course, I thought, "What are the chances of that happening?
"

But, I also left the problem to the one who, I felt, had caused it, God. I figured that if it was really a message that He wanted me to deliver, then the guy would come to me.

You see, you can take these messages back to God and ask Him what to do with them. I used to think that I needed to go to sleep to get the messages from God. That is not true. He talks in the day time as well. It's just that, sometimes we hear Him better at night.

We hear Him better at night because our flesh is asleep. We are composed of mind, body and spirit. Our mind is what we use to think and make decisions with. It's also called the soul, the seat of our emotions, our gut. Our body is that which we walk around in. We wear a garment while we are on the earth. It's called our body. You and really see the line between the soul and the body when someone is sick or approaching death. Their mind is active, while their body is weak. Having a body that doesn't move does not constrain the mind. Ask someone who is paralyzed.

Our spirit is that part of us which enables us to be eternal and commune with God. We are spiritual, but walk into the reality of it as long as we are on the earth. The spiritual nature is hidden unless we ask God to help reveal it. The spiritual forces are mysterious and unseen, yet as real as the physical and the mental aspects of who we are.

The reason we hear God better at night is that our mind is idle and our flesh is asleep, so it's the only time He has to get a word in. Often, our days are filled with our own thoughts, television, radio and incessant noise.

And, the usual way we go about our day is being led by a combination of our will and our flesh. Our will gets us out of bed when the alarm goes off because we need to go to work to pay the bills, but it is our flesh that urges us to eat the donuts in the break room on the way to our first assignment. So, we have been led by or mind and our flesh, but what about our spirit? Usually, it trails after us, hardly being recognized as we move through the day. But, often, when we pause to contemplate the day and say our prayers at night, we remember that we are spiritual beings in need of someone greater than us to help us with life's issues and guard our family.

What this provides for God is a stepping stone toward speaking to us because we have opened the door. We have put aside the other things that intrude on His time, so He claims it. That is why dreams are so powerful.

One of the ways I 'power boosted' my dreams was to listen to praise music all night. In Psalms it says that our spirit never sleeps, so I figured that if my spirit was that aspect of me that I used to praise God with, it might like to continue to praise Him, on and on. You might call it an experiment in 'nonstop praise'…I think it worked. And, when my husband is out of town, I still do it. It is amazing and wonderful how refreshed I feel when I praise God all night long!

But, let me tell you what happened with the guy that I was supposed to deliver the message to about being lazy. One day a weeks after I had the dream, he stopped me and pulled out a chair and asked me, "What's up; have you had any dreams lately?"

Well, I took this as my cue and told him my dream. He became angry and I walked away. I figured that I was relieved of my duty because, like a mailman, I had delivered my mail.

But, I felt bad as I returned to my work space and mentioned it to a person that I was working with. It was obvious that I was upset because my face was red… I prayed for the first guy and, in a few minutes decided to go back to him that he didn't need to stay the way he was if he didn't want to.

I was not prepared for what happened, because he proceeded to tell me that when he was young, his parents wanted him to be a priest, but he became disillusioned and turned his back on God. His final words to me were, "Sheri, this is your dream. If God wants to speak to me, He will give me a dream."

My response was ready because God had already told me what to say. I looked deep into his eyes and said, "Perhaps that is why He gave it to me; maybe you aren't listening." And, I walked away.

I went back to my work space with a look of shock and related as much of the story to my coworker who knew about the ordeal without revealing the identity of the person who I had delivered the message to. When I came to the part about him missing the opportunity to be a priest, the guy that I was talking to nearly passed out on his feet. He became white as a ghost. So, I said, "What is it?"

He said, "I have never told anyone this except my wife, but years ago I felt the calling to become a priest and I asked God to give me a sign if He wanted me to become one. That night I had a dream and heaven opened up and a giant hand reached out to me and beckoned to me to come. But, I ignored the dream up until now. And, who are you that you have brought this message to me?"

Seeing that he was already married and could not be a priest at this point, I asked him the question, "When does the grace of God stop?"

When he finally answered me that the grace of God never stops, I replied, "Then, what that means is if we miss our exit ramp on the freeway that we are supposed to be on, God will provide another. It

42

is never too late to do His will."

I tell you these stories to encourage you to go to God and ask Him what you should do with the dreams where He tells you things that others are doing wrong. I believe that if you are close to God, then it is kind of like bedding down with a friend; you tell one another secrets. And, sometimes, He tells me things just because He likes to talk and knows I'll listen.

It's not that I need to run over and tell the individuals messages that He has given, but it's sort of like being with your best friend and sharing information just because you're nearby.

So, when ever I get one of those dreams that say someone is 'bad' or doing something wrong, I take it back to God in the daytime and ask Him what to do with it. What helps me is to fast ahead of time, when ever I am sent to deliver a 'hard' message. I write it down and try to be as humble as I think Jesus would be. What I have found is that, more often than not, God uses the message in the dream to help turn the person around.

V. Embrace the Visual

The dream can be one that leads toward intimacy, teaching or encouragement. Intimacy draws us closer to God, teaching tells us about who He is and who we are. Encouragement uplifts our soul.

Fun with Dreams

Let's have some fun with dreams. If you have never made any attempt to interpret your dreams before now, then any attempt will be honored by God. Suppose, you are not very good at interpreting your dreams and are only able to get part of the message; let's say 30%, then that is 30% more than you have ever gotten before.

We are not under obligation to understand our dreams, but they are helpful in receiving some fun messages from God. Think of it like you are a construction worker who goes to work in the morning after his wife packs his lunch. Eventually, he will sit down in the shade and open the lunch box. Suppose, he doesn't eat his lunch that day: it's no big deal. He can take it home without eating it if he gets a meal some other way. But, suppose, there is a note from his wife tucked inside that tells him how much she loves him that day. And, suppose, for the sake of conversation, that it is a special day in their history together, such as an anniversary of a first date, or something like that. If he didn't open the lunch box, then he would never see the note left by his wife. Does he need the note to survive? No.

In the same way, we don't need to interpret our dreams to be able to survive within the grace of God living as a Child of His. But, if He is sending us a lunch at night, and there is a note inside, why not read it?

Dreams are given to us in riddles, most of the time, and we need to unwind the messages within to figure them out. Let me encourage you that I have about as many dreams that I have no figured out, as I have those I have been able to interpret. Anything is better than nothing. Dreams are like the parable of the ten talents in the Bible. The man left servants in charge of his cash and went to a distant land. He gave them all money of different amounts. It wasn't a matter of how much each had, but what they did with what they were given. So, my friend, it is not a matter of being the 'best' dream interpreter, but being willing to give it a try. And, suppose that God is trying to tell you something and you are able to unravel the mystery to obtain the answer? Believe, me, I know for sure, that there is nothing more rewarding than being able to come up with the answer, follow it and come out with a positive outcome. It is rewarding.

Here are a few pointers that may help, if you are not familiar with the Bible:

A door is something we walk through. If you have dreams with lots of doors, then there are several areas that you need to walk through. Jesus is, also, called the door to a relationship with God. Perhaps you need to get where you are going by recognizing His atonement for your sin and seeking His provision to get there. A door is similar to a road, in that it needs to be passed through to get somewhere. But, remember, a door must be walked through, not on, like a road.

A road is different. We have roads that lead us places, just like we all have paths in our lives. Jesus provides the only free way. Remember, Jesus said that He is the way, the truth and the life, no one comes to the Father except by Him. A road in your dream may have curves or climbs, or down hills. These are all indications of the road that is stretching in front of you. It indicates the path that is before you. Are you on a wide road or a skinny road? Remember, the road is wide that leads to destruction, but narrow that leads to eternal life.

Suppose you are on a path with a lot of rocks or impediments, I could mean that there are many problems in your way. But, it could also mean that there are issues in your life that you are tripping over. Remember, that Jesus is a stone of stumbling to some, but others use Him to climb on to other things.

Windows are ways to see through things. There are windows to heaven and windows into our soul. They can be ways we see God and ways we see others. Remember that the windows of heaven were opened and God rained. His reign happens when the windows of heaven are opened in our lives.

Many times people tell me about a dream where they are climbing. We climb up to God, remember? He is up and we are down here on earth. Climbing could mean upward momentum toward His ways, rather than our own.

Houses usually are us. We are the residence of the Holy Spirit. When Jesus ascended into heaven He gave us the Holy Spirit and He takes up residence within our soul when we ask Him to. We have a front door, a back door and areas where we sleep. We have regions of cleansing and where we eat. A house can also indicate places of worship or the house of God. It is a place of residence.

Walls are partitions between rooms. Perhaps you have built up some walls in your life that are keeping things out. There are positive walls and negative walls. Certainly, we would not like the Devil to come into our house, freely. There are inner walls and outer walls. The inner walls have to do with our inner self and the outer walls can indicate the barriers that we are putting up in our relationship with others. There are walls around buildings and castles to protect them. There are also walls around our houses to keep us safe. Walls are an extensive study within the Bible and you can search them on your own, if you find that you are having a lot of dreams on walls.

Death in a dream is interesting. Many people get very upset when they dream about someone and they die. They are afraid that it is prophetic and that their loved one will die. I disagree. I do not think God gives us many, if any, dreams that indicate we, or others will die.

Occasionally, I have seen individuals have a dream that

protected them from an situation that could have been harmful. For, example: a car wreck. When the person had a dream about having a car wreck, she drove very carefully the next day. She did end up in a wreck but, she was not injured as in the dream, and she supposed that it was because that she heeded the warning within the dream.

I have found that what death usually means is that someone has died to something. Let me explain. Every day, when we are walking in the grace of God, we die to our own desires and live to His. We put aside our flesh and seek spiritual goals. We die to our old self and live to our new self. It is like baptism, in a way: we are dead to our old ways and risen to new life in Christ. We put aside the things of the world and take up the things of God. We die to sin and live to righteousness. You see? There are many areas where we can die, so it is not unusual to think that we die daily. That is what Paul says in the New Testament. (Colossians 2.20, I Corinthians 15).

The first time a friend came to me and told me that he had a disturbing dream that I had died, I laughed. Because, the day prior, I had been hiking in the desert and laid on a rock as a symbol to God that I would give myself as a living sacrifice to Him. I saw this flat rock and thought it was a good time to re commit my life to Him. In essence, I died to doing things my own way and I was reborn to doing things His way. He gave me rebirth into His new way of thinking after I was willing to lay down and die for Him. By my friend having this dream, God was simply telling him that I was making a big commitment in my life to Him.

A brother in a dream can mean your physical brother, or it can mean your brothers and sisters in Christ at the Church. Try to expand your vision when you view dreams.

A sister can also mean the same. The message could be for your sister, but probably is for all of your sisters in Christ telling you how to behave with others.

There is a lot of water in dreams. Water is interesting. It can mean a lot of things. When you are at the sea, it usually means that you 'see' something. But, remember, that the Holy Spirit is also described as flowing water.

So, is it where we meet the Holy Spirit that we 'see' things? I could be. You float on the sea and you can walk on the sea. With the floating, you need a vehicle, like a boat, but with the walking, you use your feet. Does God want you to use your gifts (vehicles) to get where He is sending you, or does He want you to simply use faith to get there?

Believers in God are trees in the Bible. That doesn't mean that every time you see a tree in your dream that you are in the midst of believers. It could mean that you are in the midst of an area where you can't see clearly where you are going. But, perhaps there are others in your way. Ask questions to God and He will answer you.

There is a mountain of prayer, as there is a closet of prayer. There are avenues of prayer and there is a place like a porch that is a place of prayer.

Dreams about someone who is dead are dependent on your relationship with that person. If your mother is dead, then perhaps God is showing you comfort in her passing. But, often, I have seen that our mother is used as an example of 'mother wisdom in heaven'. She could be like a mentor in your dreams to teach you principles about the Kingdom of God.

Dreams about others that are dead could be teaching you about the Kingdom of Heaven. If the individual is in heaven, then God is setting the scene by putting them in heaven within the dream. He sets the scene then paints the picture. What He means for you to do is compare the Kingdom of heaven with the Kingdom here on earth.

He puts someone you know is in heaven within your dream, then gives a scenario to teach you a lesson.

Dreams about your father, regardless of whether he is dead or alive, usually are related to your heavenly father. He uses the only example of a father that you may have within your life in an attempt to teach you something about His character. He doesn't usually show up, Himself within the dream, but sends a representative with a message.

Sometimes when there are several characters in a dream, all of them are you. For example, I had a dream last night and I was the same as I am today. Then, there was a little girl in the dream, as well. I think that I am also the little girl in the dream. For the sake of understanding I will tell you the dream:

I am on a boat with my husband and we go down a canal. There are many hazards in the water along the way, but I stand on the bow and look into the water pointing them out so we won't run into them with the boat as we come into the shallow water. We are making way to put the boat to shore. Then, the dream clips to a little girl. I bring her into the house and she wants to stay. I am worried she might be alone there, but then I notice mom. I can feel safe to leave her to mom's care. I wonder why I haven't trusted her before? She has been there all along, yet I never noticed her before.

OK, Here is the interpretation that I got from this dream:

God, as my husband; the one who tends me, is bringing this boat ashore. He is bringing the idea of interpretation of dreams ashore. There have been obstacles along the way, but as I have looked with my spiritual eyes through the power of the Holy Spirit, He has pointed out the hazards to me and I have been able to not run aground prematuraly.

But, now is the time.

A second message of the dream begins with the second clip. I believe the little girl in the dream is me. Mom refers to mother Wisdom. She has been there all along for me and will continue to be there for me. Just because I haven't noticed her all the time, doesn't mean she hasn't been there for me. So, the dream is one of reassurance. Indeed, both the woman and the girl in the dream are me.

There are dreams where God talks. I have had dreams where He taps me on the shoulder and interprets the dream at the time I am dreaming it. Any words embedded within the dream are important. They provide the key to unlocking the dream. Usually, you can't figure out how the words related to the pictures, but if you take them back to the Bible and ask God, in prayer how they relate, He will tell you.

Three types of dream interpretation:

!. Basic Interpretation

The first one is basic interpretation. With this type anyone can do it. write down the dream and look at the words. Then, focus on correlations between the words. For example, a fishing line may be a way to haul things in, but it also may be something to read. It may be a way to catch a person that we think need to be saved, but it also may be a demarcation between two areas.

With basic dream interpretation the individual needs to write down the dream in as much detail as possible. Omit any outside details in your life. Do not allow them to enter into the dream interpretation or they will cause a skew in the results. Use a piece of paper to write down the dream so that you can look at the words.

Then, step back. Sometimes, I don't come back to the words for a few hours. It is important not to get too sidetracked with the images within the dreams. The images are given to convey a message. For example, a pink house in a dream could be looked at too closely and cause problems.

If you told me that you had a dream with a pink house in it, I would say that the house was 'bright, or loud'. Pink is a bright color. So, with this house, which usually is an individual, he is bright our loud. Don't get sidetracked on peripheral issues like, 'Does it mean that he's gay because the house is pink?'

You see how that leads you down a whole different road. Maybe the individual is gay, but I would ask God for confirmation on that question. That is another issue: you can always ask God for confirmation on the interpretation of a dream.

Remember, there is another night coming soon. If it is an important message, then He will be happy to confirm the message for you so that you can get it. Often, when I ask God questions, He gives me three for four dreams in the same night to confirm the messages.

After you have written it down and stood back from the words, then ask question of the dream. For example, if there is a river, then why isn't it a lake? If there are only red tulips, why are there not other flowers? Ask questions and list them on paper, then answer them one by one asking God. You will find that He will drop the answers into your soul because He wants the mystery unraveled for you.

Try to summarize the meaning of the dream into a few sentences, so that you can take it with you. It will mean more. When I write dreams in the night on a pad, I look over them the next morning and add any words that I may have left out, but can still remember in the morning. It helps when I don't get to it to interpret it until later.

2. Prophetic Interpretation

The second level of dream interpretation is that of prophecy This area of prophecy is related to impending events. I believe that we have some dreams that tell us of events that are going to come about before hand. This area is very tenuous, however, because, it is difficult to know when the dream will be fulfilled.

We need to be careful to not end up like Joseph in the Old Testament. When he had a dream that indicated that his brothers were going to bow down to him, he told them and they became jealous of him and sold him to gypsies.

So, you need to be careful with these types of dreams, so your friends and families don't sell you to gypsies.

3. A Teaching

The third level of dream interpretation is where you are able to break your own persona out of the picture and see the lesson in it apart from you personally. This takes a lot of practice and study in the Scriptures. What you do is attempt to relate all of the words to the Bible. You separate the pictures from the words and keep the words, only. The Father becomes 'Our Father' and the 'son' becomes 'Jesus' or 'Children of God'. If you can learn to separate the principle from the direction for your personal life, then the dream will be able to become useful for others.

Let's do some dreams. I have put examples of each type of dream within this book to give a flavor of what to do with them.

Use the structure:

Build on the Matrix of the dream Sometimes when we look at the dream, it looks like we have been given a ball of yarn and need to knit it together to make a picture. Some aren't very good at knitting, so let me help you out. Dreams are a lot like knitting in that there are colored threads that weave through giving rise to ideas. When you think of dreams, think of ideas, not things, and you will do better.

Here is an example: A fellow came to me and asked me what could this dream mean?

When I was in Junior High I had this dream every night right when I went to sleep. I dreamt that I was falling into a volcano.

Let me show you how easy this is to interpret. If you begin with writing the dream down, it always helps. Then, define the words. A volcano is something unpredictable what erupts without notice sending destruction to all in its path. Simple definition.

So, I asked him, "When you were in Junior High, was there someone or something that was always in danger of erupting without notice sending destruction and devastation to all in its path?"

And, he replied, "Oh yes. It was me. I had a terrible problem with anger when I was in Junior High." See how easy that was. To him this dream was important because the night before he met me, he had the dream again and was worried that the dreams would start up again just like they had in Junior High.

My response was, "I guess you need to resolve your anger problem. Talk with God."

Use Binoculars

Use binoculars to focus on the island.

Dreams are like a painting on the wall, if you stand too close to it, you won't be able to see the whole picture. If you get too into 'detail' then you won't pick up the main message because you will be too sidetracked. Think of it this way: If you have a painting you hang it on the wall across the room and look at it from a distance. If there are details in the painting that catch your eye, then you step closer and take a look. You focus on colors or textures after you have grasped the original message.

The way I think of them is like looking at a dessert island with binoculars. First, you have to find the island, then; you can focus on the landscape and the beach. After that you can begin to see if it has birds or coconuts. But, it wouldn't work to begin looking for coconuts when you don't have the island in your field of vision. The same is with a dream: you need to know the subject of the dream before you can focus on the message of it.

Suppose the dream is about a little girl who is brought into a bank and sat on a counter by her governess. The woman declares to the owner of the bank that she can't get the girl to do anything because he must first write it down. Then, as he begins to write, the little girl hops over the counter and climbs onto his lap watching his hand as it forms the letters telling her to go home and take a bath.

So, what is the subject of the dream above? Let me show you what happens if you do any of the three things that are backwards. Watch, I will do the dream three times, leaving the right interpretation for the final analysis:

a. will focus on the details of the dream: The dream is about a little girl who is spoiled. She needs discipline after all, her 'governess' puts her on the counter and she runs to her father who has to write her instructions because she won't go take a bath. So, the interpretation could be: Do I have to tell you when to take a bath? God clean up.

    <u>b.</u> Let's do the dream again, focusing on the message instead of the subject: I will be going to a bank sometime soon and the owner will write notes. After all, I am a child of the King. Others will wait on me and I will be shown preference.

    <u>c.</u> Let's try it again attempting to focus on the subject first. Remember, a sentence is no good without a subject. Find the subject. If you can't find the subject, then ask for clarification before you launch out with advice that isn't good. So, to find the subject, I ask questions: Who is who and what does a bank represent? Well, I think the girl is me and the bank represents what I bank on. Where do I bank? What do I lean on for support? In the dream it isn't a place that I go to on my own, but am delivered to by someone who is in charge of me.

I bank on the promises of God because they have been brought to me, and I have been brought to them; and certainly my father is there amidst them.

You see, the dream doesn't have anything to do with finances or with getting clean. What it has to do with is watching God write out the details of my life sitting on His lap because I am His child.

When you get a dream, try to back up from it, removing the words from the pictures. In the dream above, if I said, "I bank on the hand that stands behind where the riches are invested. It is that hand which I see at work." This statement would be true because it correlates with Scripture. You see, there is no 'right' answer as long as it correlates with Scriptures. The first interpretation doesn't match up with Scriptures because in the dream the girl doesn't do anything wrong. She just doesn't want to take a bath because her father hasn't told her to.

The second interpretation is even further off center in that God has called us to put others above us, not look to get money from them.

You must back way up and look at what you have: a girl, a dad and someone who brings her there. Then, when you figure out who is who, you can move on to what they are doing and why. Only then, can you deduct the message.

Catch the vision: focus

Remember, a dream is an impression, not reality. Often the message is imbedded in the impression that you got when you were put in the situation. Be sure to write down your feelings and ideas at the time during the dream. Suppose you have a dream you are in a car that is heading down a road in the dessert with your friends. Then, you have a dreadful feeling of impending doom and all of a sudden the car is flying across the sky and lands in a hay stack.

Your feeling is that you were going to crash when you were in the dream. But, within the dream, you don't. In fact, you make a safe, soft landing.

Let's back up from this dream and interpret it. I think you will be able to get it. First, look at the central message:
- You are not alone
- But, you feel something is going to go wrong
- You sail through the air.
- Thereis a safe landing.

So unravel it: Guess what, God is your constant companion. Even when you don't feel like it. He is the one who provides for the safe landings in this 'era'. He says, 'Hay, come on over to My side. I know about softness."

See, the words had hidden messages in them as well; Air could bc cra, hay as in straw, became hay, as a word of invitation invoked by a friend.

So, the central message is: "I know you are insecure and afraid. Don't worry I will be beside you and provide a safe haven."

In short, " Relax. Fly to God's hey stack"

Glimpse of the Print

Suppose you desire to catch some of these 'gold threads' of God's wisdom coming down from heaven, but aren't sure the best way to do it.

First, you have to write the dream down. It's very hard to retain dream information without writing it down.

I write the dreams down in the middle of the night with a dark pen so I don't write over my self. I don't turn the light on. I tried to use light pens, but they didn't work for me. They were too bright and 'woke' me up from the dream and I couldn't remember it.

Sometimes, I can only catch the 'just' of the message and can't remember any of the details. But, it's surprising, that in the morning when I wake up and read my notebook, how profound these simple messages are.

You wouldn't believe how many times, God has come to me with a simple message saying it over and over; I wake up and think, "This is soo easy, certainly I will remember it in the morning." But, then I can't.

And, I think that, even though God gives messages and leading through dreams, they are not the primary mode of delivery for everyone. There are individuals who may only have a few dreams while others are bombarded with them. What is most important is what you do with them when you receive them. Certainly, you don't want to be left praying and praying for an answer, only to find you received it in a dream wrapped message that you failed to open. That brings me to another issue: answers to prayer.

VI. Problems with Focus

Dirty lens

Sometimes when we strain to see the island, we can't focus on it because our lens is full of smudges. We need to take out a lens cloth and clean it so we can see better. If there is dirt and grime in your life, clean it up. If there is sin, confess it. The good thing about God is that He is open 24 hours a day for us to talk to Him. It's just that, sometimes we can't hear His voice because there are too many things between His and where we are. He provides the option for us to come to His arena. Don't think for a moment that you can drag God into your grimy world, because He is a Holy God who can't stand in the presence of sin.

So, if you are having problems with understanding the matrix of dreams, but sincerely want to, ask God what stands between you and Him. He will tell you and when He does, copy it down and do it. Then, turn around and you will find the answer to your question. It was just grime on the lens.

Dream Reruns

Rerun dreams are those dreams that we dream over and over. They can be annoying, especially if we don't know what they mean.

There are two main reasons why dreams are repeated. One is that the message is important; it's worth repeating. Like an anniversary. It's worth celebrating over and over because it is important.

The second main reason is that we aren't getting the message. Often, dreams are like an EKG. An EKG is a picture of the heart that is electrical tracings. They place leads all over the chest and take a simultaneous picture from 12 different views. It's the same heart, just different pictures from different angles to give more information for the doctor to make the best diagnosis possible. Dreams are like this: Often we receive the same message, only from different angles to help us understand the meaning better. If you are having the same dream over and over, then you need to stop and look at it. Perhaps it is a warning of some danger that is impending. Chances are, however, that you have had several dreams in between the two that are the same, that are like messages from different angles, like an EKG.

How can I get them to stop?

The way that you can get rerun dreams to stop is to pay attention to them. When you respond to the message, then you will be ready for a new message. If the one that God is trying to send you is extremely important, then, He will keep sending it, to try to protect you. Think of your brain like an eraser board. The teacher is God's wisdom. If the assignment is important for you to do to be able to move on to the next level, then, He will keep giving it to you each time you enter the room the next day. (Or as this case may be, at night when you go to sleep.)

Falling asleep in the Movie

Dreams come like a fragrance; an essence. They are not substance in that you can't reach out and touch them, yet no one can deny their existence. Often, they are the closest we can come to God. Many dream about heaven and hell and spirits. They have dreams of falling and falling, or going through door after door. They have symbolism of eternal things.

Dreams come like a smell. We are the only one what can determine what it smells like to us. To one it may smell like the perfume worn by their mother and to another it may smell like the flowers in the back yard. The dream takes on new meaning according to the meaning to the individual.

Sometimes, we can't remember all of the details of the dream; we can still remember the essence, or the smell of it. That's OK because, maybe that is what we need. For instance, I couldn't remember any of the aspects of the adventure, but my husband was with me. Well, for me the message was, "Your husband is with you."

That may seem like a pert answer, but at the time it was important because I was spending hours in my study working on these books and was wondering if my husband was 'with me' in the venture. This dream brought assurance by the fragrance of it, not the content of it.

Dreams Unanswered

And a dream is just a dream
until you see it as so much more
And a dream unfulfilled will never come ashore.

A dream left unanswered
is one only given at night.
It tickles the emotions
but is not brought to the light.

For a dream must be carried out in the daytime,
To be worked out and shown to be true.
And a dream that is unraveled can become more
than between me and you.

The dreams of our heart
often mix with those from above
They are scattered with gold dust,
encouragement and God's love.

VII. The Matrix Template

CAEFA
Capitulate, associate,
emulate,
facilitate, and appreciate.

I have developed a practice template for you. It can't hurt for you to try to figure out your dream. The worse thing you can do is come up with the wrong message. What I have done is made a deal with God: When I come up with the wrong message, then He can fix it with another dream the next night. But, the other side of this deal is that I have to be faithful to copy them all down.

You see, if I mess up in dream number 3 of a 10 part series and then I fail to copy down number 4, the whole message is out of whack. So, I leave these deals with God up to you. I only mention them, because the area of dreams is risky business and there is no 'right' answer.

I maintain that there are a lot of 'right' answers that go with a single dream when we take time to figure it out. The questions on this dream test are all 'essay' so everyone has a chance and it doesn't matter how wordy you get. There are no right and wrong boxes to check. And, no one else can tell you if your interpretation is wrong or not, unless it does not correlate with Scripture. There are several 'right' answers to the same dream. I go back to the same dream over and over, if it is a profound one that has made a deep impression. A dream is like a box delivered to our doorstep; we need to turn it over and see that there are more stamps on the other side. We can recycle them over and over and get new messages. I challenge you to try.

If you have a 'Nintendo level 10' dream and you need help

with it, you can access our www.fordreamers.com web site where there is an active dream chat room. I will break in there and help interpret as many as I can.

CAEFA

Capitulate: Surrender to His ways and summarize subject.

Associate: Connect with Him having subordinate status.

Emulate: Compete for the answer. Vie for the truth against all else.

Facilitate: Make it easy and convenient. Ask and write it down.

Appreciate: Become fully aware of the value; to be sensitive to and show gratitude for with an increase in proportionate value to that which is revealed. It's OK to say, "Thanks."

What does it say?

Copy the words and feelings.

Define any words.

Be sure to check for double meaning or words that sound similar. (i.e. 'are a' and 'era', 'red dress' and 'redress', 'hole' and 'whole')If the dream says you're in a hole, it could mean you can't get out of where you are, or it could mean you are complete.

Define the subject.

There is no use continuing with the dream until you know the subject. Consider that it is a message that God wants to deliver to you. He will help clarify it if you ask. Some dreams I have taken to the dessert and went on a 5 hour hike just to figure out. Be patient.

What does it mean?

What is the message of the dream? What is it trying to say?

What is the purpose of the dream?

Why would you receive this message? If it is a message for someone else, why was it given to you? To warn, protect or as a message to deliver? What am I to do about it? Think of it like a father would talk to his son; There is a reason why he would tell him something. There should be a response from us when wc are given a message. Remember, our response needs to align with Scriptures as well as the interpretation. God would not have us belittle our brother or curse our mother.

Put the Kingdom of God in the center.

If the message is from Him, then it is His ideas, not yours. Try to begin to discern which thoughts are yours and which are His. I will give you a clue: His are holy. Remove yourself from the center of the focus, think bigger. It will help if your focus begins with the subject of the dream, not you. Don't presume that you are always the star of these movies.

How dreams come to pass

When we have dreams given by God, there will be spiritual opposition to the dream. The dream will always have obstacles to being birthed. We must envision the dream, then step out by faith believing it to be true, then move. The first part of a step is to determine to move that direction. Then part is to lift your foot in that direction. At that point your face and your body are in union toward the motion. The third step is to continue to move.

When we speak of spiritual dreams we need to establish victory within the spiritual realm before we can think to have victory in the physical arena. We need to go from the valley of Giants to the place of victory. We wrestle against principalities and powers, not against flesh and blood. So, when we are successful in our spiritual conquest, we will automatically have victory in the things evident.

As Jesus called Peter out of the boat to walk on the water, it was by faith that he was able to stand in a place where others would surely sink. When He gives us a vision, or a dream, and we pray for the conquest of the victory, then we must walk toward the enemy in the direction of the land that God wants us to conquer. We can pray and pray, but if we never walk, then we have not moved by faith to believe in God's word for victory.

Often, I assist people to pray for their loved ones for healing. As I do, I notice something. They pray for healing, yet do not give God the opportunity to do it. For, if we pray for God to enable someone to breath on their own, yet never remove him from the respirator, or even turn it down, then how will we know that he is healed.

Also, when we pray for healing, sometimes it takes time. I have seen people pray for healing, then, stop the machines that sustain life the very next day. I have wondered if they asked God about Hs timing for healing. Perhaps another day, and the Lord would have turned their loved one's condition around to promote healing. When we pray, we need to begin walking in the direction of the answer.   It is then, that God will make it safer for us to walk on the water than in the boat. We are protected when we walk by faith, not when we don't. Peter was called out to walk on the water. If he did not walk, where was he? He was in the midst of disbelief.

So, if God shows us a dream, and we pray in that direction, it becomes safer to walk on the water, move out in faith, than to stay in the boat. For, when we are on the water, walking within the faith of the dream, we will be walking toward the provision of Hs dream.

I Chronicles 21, Isaiah 51.6.

{Taken from Firefly, a book on how to get the words from your dreams. GBB not yet done.}

In conclusion, there are only a few things that we need, day or night to hear the voice of God: We need to learn to quiet our heart to the noise of the world, our flesh and our own minds; we need to purify our thoughts to align with His, and we need to release our spirit to join with His Spirit. It's spiritual unity which enables us to hear God.

Then, finally, we need to get ready. Because when God sees that someone is willing to listen, He talks. So, you had better have a piece of paper. Caëfa

Adendum
My Caëfa{Cache of Dreams}

Hi jacked Dream

If I don't understand, sometimes I hold up the dream with a pocket knife. I threaten it myself, to kill it.

I hijack my own air liner to try to bring it down to where I think it should go.

My destination. We are hijacking the Word of God; the direction for our lives mid stream and threatening total destruction. If all the passages end up at the wrong destination, with the wrong tutor like scriptures or words of direction we all have a ticket.

One of our own direction. We've landed on a runway too short not meant to be where we've gone. But it was hard. There was fog and bad weather. So, we turned on our own GPS. But, we couldn't see out the window.

We've spent too much time reflecting on our own thoughts, like looking at ourselves in the mirror. We only notice how imperfect we are. So, we pass out our little mirrors to the whole plane load of paying passengers all going our direction.

They start looking at their own image of who God is and what He wants them to do. All the while they have been hijacked by our own ideas. But, we held the knife, the Word to their throat. We have embezzled people like money. We've skimmed for ourselves the prophet. We have stolen from God what was rightfully His. He wants to grow His people, His way, in His time. We need to disembark and unload, abandon our own program.

But in our mind it is huge. 707 full of people. But, our program is doomed to run out of gas because we never calculated and factored in if I have enough to get there. Because we were not part of the original planning session, the gas in the plane may not equal the trip because now we have taken it to a place it was not meant to go.

We have hi jacked it to going our own way. That five finger thing we need to put our hands in our pockets and learn to be quiet before God. Less work and more listen.

We forget the other side of the I when we trail out on our own vision. He lives to provide us with one. It's the US vision. You, me and Him. US. The Son is the GPS, ATV reflecting His glory because we receive His signal and send it back. We've become a reliable relay.

Like a glass insulator along a wire we take what He gives and send it down the line. We are not to change what He gives, just to sent it down the line. Its the electric fence. Power contained and maintained by Him for a specific purpose. Maintain the Wall; the fence.

His walls of our thinking. Our walls have turned the power off. We thought the electric fence was unsafe, out of control, unreliable, unpredictable, out of date and not what we need for now. But we are wrong. The insulators are beautiful relays. They are blue glass and they are perfect for what He needs.

Understanding the voice of God
October 21, 2005

Hear and Hold

I started out showing them how to preserve a single word because I knew there would be adversity all along. If they could understand and hold onto one word, then they could work up to more.

Hear and hold against all odds: cling
Understand
Work up to more

Dreams without Interpretation

Sometimes I can't figure out the interpretation of a
dream it's because it has not been given to me.
It is not that He doesn't want me to know the
answer, but, it requires more
than my thinking.
I must take the dream back to
Him and ask for answers. Then, He will give
them to me. I must call on his love in addition
to His gifts of wisdom, understanding,
knowledge, might, fear of the Lord,
presence, and counsel.
He will speak
as I
listen
and rely
upon Him. He wants
me to understand and grow with Him.
I proclaim the same at night as in the day
to bring to light the things now hidden in darkness.

Revolutionist

The Dream: He was a black activist and he had been shot several times. The car is all shot up. The body was riddled with bullets and hanging out of the car door. The debate is whether or not he is dead. He sure looks dead to me. I wonder why they even debate?

Interpretation: There is someone dark who is activating a movement. At this time he is riddled with bullets. And, they wonder if he is dead?

Dreams of the night are riddled with bullets from God. They are wondering if hearing messages from God through dreams is dead. When I look at what they have done to the wisdom of God, no wonder they think hearing God through dreams is dead. They have tried to shoot so many holes into this way God carries His bulletins, that, no wonder, they wonder. The world has attempted to totally shoot down all of this movement of God.

First, they shoot holes into the vehicle: How could a dream be reliable? Certainly, dreams are from our own imagination. Can words of God come from imagination? If they are from your imagination, then they are not from God. They are from you.

Then, they shoot holes into the window: How do you know who God is? What is your image of God? If God is outside of where we live, then what makes you think that He wants to invade our world?

Then, there are theological arguments: What makes you think you can see God? If nobody has seen Him like this, what makes you think that you can, now? Certainly, you need education from Bible Schools and pastoral institutions to think that you are able to discern and understand words from God. Are you sure God speaks outside of the Scriptures? The Bible says that Scripture is closed when the Bible was completed. Are you adding to the Word of God?

And, what makes you think that your windows are clean enough to see the things of God? If you are not pure, then how do you think you can hear from a pure God? Oh, man who are you to think you can talk with God: not to God, but with God?

Then, they shot holes in the person who actively carried the message and attempted to tell others. He is a revolutionist. And what is that? He is someone who believes a message and is willing to stand up for it and live it. When this person speaks, he causes a rumble and defuses the theories of the world. He is certainly a threat to them. The reason they would want to get rid of him is because: when others listen to him, then they will ask God and God will talk. When God talks, He might have something bad to say about those who promoted wrong thinking. They will loose their supporters.

The world wants to hold people in bondage, just like slavery. That is why the person in the dream is like a black activist; because he is promoting something that is not popular, but true.

Just like me.

And, the flip side is that this person is the worldly thinking regarding dreams. This has been totally shot down. There is a new revolution now and the old one is dead. God is leading the way with His new thinking. The darkness of the night has been shot down: old ways of knowing dreams has been shot down, without a doubt. There is no question that God is speaking through dreams.

October 15, 2005

Unity in Training

October 5, 2005

And, nobody understands how this grew from that. How did I figure it out? How did I figure out the dreams?

So, we take instructions on how to do things. I know they got it from by books. Others follow the instructions on in.

We are all in training. Some dine at one place and some dine at the other. I gather them all up to eat together. Unity is ultimate, not which restaurant we eat at. Then, we go to class. It's fun. I race others for the lot. Where the vehicles are parked there is danger. A crane is moving them from above. They could very well fall on us. Others help those stuck in the mud. And, they have big boulders they are craning around. A rock falls on us. It has been hallowed out (hallowed be thy name) inside to provide us with space. Still, why do they move these rocks when there are people below? It's unsafe. We only had barely enough breathing room. A channel of air was provided when we got on our hands and knees.

This is a book: Lighthearted interpretation of dreams.

He didn't bring me new provision. He just opened my eyes to see how to use what was already in my hand. When the rock falls on us, and we find the center there is only room and air for two on your hands and knees. You become the diamond within the rock. You are the gem that lives within as He brings you through the circumstances.

I come from one spiritual background and others come from theirs. It doesn't matter what our spiritual orientation is, God can move us to the place where He will train us. It is important for us all to come together to dine at His table. It is His presence that the interpretation or our lives and dreams comes together.

When circumstances happen that we don't

understand, He will enable us to interpret them when He hits us with the rock of His knowledge. He is the rock, the firm foundation and the sure way. He is the protection. There is only room for two, because when we enter into the rock, we will find that He is there with us, enabling us to overcome all of the obstacles that have come against us. He will provide a channel for His dreams which have become ours when we enter into His purposes. One of His purposes is to bring His Children together and teach them from His own mouth. Like gathering the kids for bedtime stories: Dad wants to read to us.

Lighthearted interpretation of dreams {This title became changed to A Dream Matrix Manual}.

Sleeping with God

The place where his patience slept was always made to accommodate Him, but He wasn't comfortable.

No one seemed to notice how big He was until I came along. I merely noticed and engaged the power of God to enlarge His presence with in the realization of dreams.

When I enlarged His presence, He pushed the enemy right out of that place. He was put under His feet. Now the space is enlarged to His right size. When we see Him as He truly is, then we will realize our view has been too small. It has been put within our hand to call upon the power and provision of God to change our image of His presence with our dreams.

His dreams can become ours through His strength. Then, we can call upon His power and demonstrate obedience walking into the words and message given. We must take our hands out of our pockets and accept assignments to care for His needs as well as ours.

We enter into a relationship of mutual tending. He tends us and we tend Him.

What happens next is that the power of God works to enlarge the area of His work within our lives. Satan is not put under our feet, but God's feet.

Often in our minds we had set up a nice place for Satan to sleep next to us. We have been complacent in defeat of our dreams. But, now we can claim the victory through the provision of God. Satan is no longer comfortable at our house sleeping in our bed. So it is crowded. To alleviate the crowding, we elevate God. He does not sleep shoulder to shoulder with the devil in dreams. The devil would have you to believe they are on the same plane and able to direct your thoughts easily. Not so, we are the ones who have allowed this thinking to cloud our picture of who God is. The screen of our mind was built to accommodate Gods pictures above any of those by the enemy. We just never noticed before.

After School Class

There is advanced dream interpretation for those who are more spiritual. They push God: press on Him.

Dream and visions for life planning

We are given dreams and visions into our lives to provide us with goals and plans helping to bring about the desires of our heart. These dreams are different from the ones we have at night, yet many of us treat them the same.

Some Dream More

Some dream more than others because a hungry open heart can never be satisfied because the open end keeps draining the love out the other side into the lap there. Like an individual with a sweet tooth, they are always hungry, but skinny.

Truth Decapitates

Truth decapitates the thought process from the flesh we live in. Ideas drive momentum. If Satan can control our ideas, he can steer out body. His ideas drive our flesh. Be careful when you feel the first tug toward something in your flesh.

Push Pins

Light bright, pictures in the night to us: dreams come. Simple and childlike just like the push pins on a picture. God draws the design for us, and then He uses it to push us.

Coordinated Effort

It is a coordinated effort between the Father, the Son and the Holy Spirit that enables us to live in the world, not be of the world, and have victory every step of the way. Jesus gave us new birth. It is the Father's Kingdom, and the Holy Spirit is our counselor.

Reruns

Repeat God's love and send it on down the line. Be a repeat receiver.

Getting the Message

Getting the message from the dream is easy. The words are written on the back of your eyes. Close your eyes and open your heart.

In the Way

Some have more visions than others because the door can't open when we are standing in front of the elevator. We are in the way of that which would take us up to the higher levels.

Contemplation of Beyond

You ask; how is God involved in dreams?
Contemplation of beyond starts now.
We have become a door to the future when
we insert the key into the slot of the door
of the house He has left us the deed to.

A Few Strands

If you can't remember the dream just grab a few strands of gold. A few strands are better than none. Save what you can. It falls from heaven.

Fill the Basket

The dreams are like colored threads that are in a basket beside a chair in front of a fire. She can take them out from the basket and use them to weave when ever she wants if they are available.

Agnostic

And, is God not the Father of both the good and the bad? Because we refuse to claim our Father does not make Him go away.

Confirmation Bridge

Confirmation is for those who are not sure. Faith bridges the gap between insecurity and getting where we need to be. God is always happy to confirm Hi word. Don't be afraid to ask for confirmation.

Energized Vision

Energize His images. Hop into the television. Climb into the view box then show and tell-a-vision to others.

Our Keys

Nobody gives another the keys and only God, Himself, can teach us how to use them.

Night Vision

Lite brite
Thru the nite (knight)
You reign with me.

Bring Heaven Down

I pray and I bring heaven down. There is a vehicle for formal dictation where we copy what He tells us. Get in and shut the door.

Dream dancing with Dad

My soul danced last night.
I am not sure of the tune and can't remember the lines.
The dance floor is a blur, but this morning my heart pines.
For, the dance was a draw, a lure from above
that twirled with my mind and showed me some love.

Like a child with her father, we danced the night away.
My shoes over His, gave me the sway.
He led the steps, His arms around mine
and sang into my ear most of the time.

But, it bothers me yet, as I lie here and fret.
Unknown to my mind is the tune of any kind.
Was it a waltz, a polka, or a glide?

My mental muscles are sore to be sure
from the miles of dance floor that was the lure.

Still, my mind is a blur, my brain is a fog,
 Recall I cannot, I must have slept like a log.
 Because, I know I danced, I twirled and I swung
for, this morning, my soul to His is brung.
We must have been close as we danced cheek to cheek
 twirled through my mind, in my heart He did peek.

But, where did we go, I wish I knew.
But, that's OK, because I think I grew
closer to my Father,
with each step.
 My shoes over His, on my pillow I slept.

August 30, 2005

dream
books

Made in the USA
Columbia, SC
31 July 2019